NEW YORK GIANTS

KENNY ABDO

abdobooks.com

Published by Abdo Zoom, a division of ABDO, P.O. Box 398166, Minneapolis, Minnesota 55439. Copyright © 2022 by Abdo Consulting Group, Inc. International copyrights reserved in all countries. No part of this book may be reproduced in any form without written permission from the publisher. Fly!™ is a trademark and logo of Abdo Zoom.

Printed in the United States of America, North Mankato, Minnesota.
052021
092021

Photo Credits: Getty Images, iStock, Shutterstock PREMIER
Production Contributors: Kenny Abdo, Jennie Forsberg, Grace Hansen
Design Contributors: Candice Keimig, Neil Klinepier

Library of Congress Control Number: 2020919502

Publisher's Cataloging-in-Publication Data

Names: Abdo, Kenny, author.
Title: New York Giants / by Kenny Abdo
Description: Minneapolis, Minnesota : Abdo Zoom, 2022 | Series: NFL teams | Includes online resources and index.
Identifiers: ISBN 9781098224745 (lib. bdg.) | ISBN 9781098225681 (ebook) | ISBN 9781098226152 (Read-to-Me ebook)
Subjects: LCSH: New York Giants (Football team)--Juvenile literature. | National Football League--Juvenile literature. | Football teams--Juvenile literature. | American football--Juvenile literature. | Professional sports--Juvenile literature.
Classification: DDC 796.33264--dc23

TABLE OF CONTENTS

NEW YORK GIANTS

Since the 1920s, the New York Giants have had a big presence on the football field.

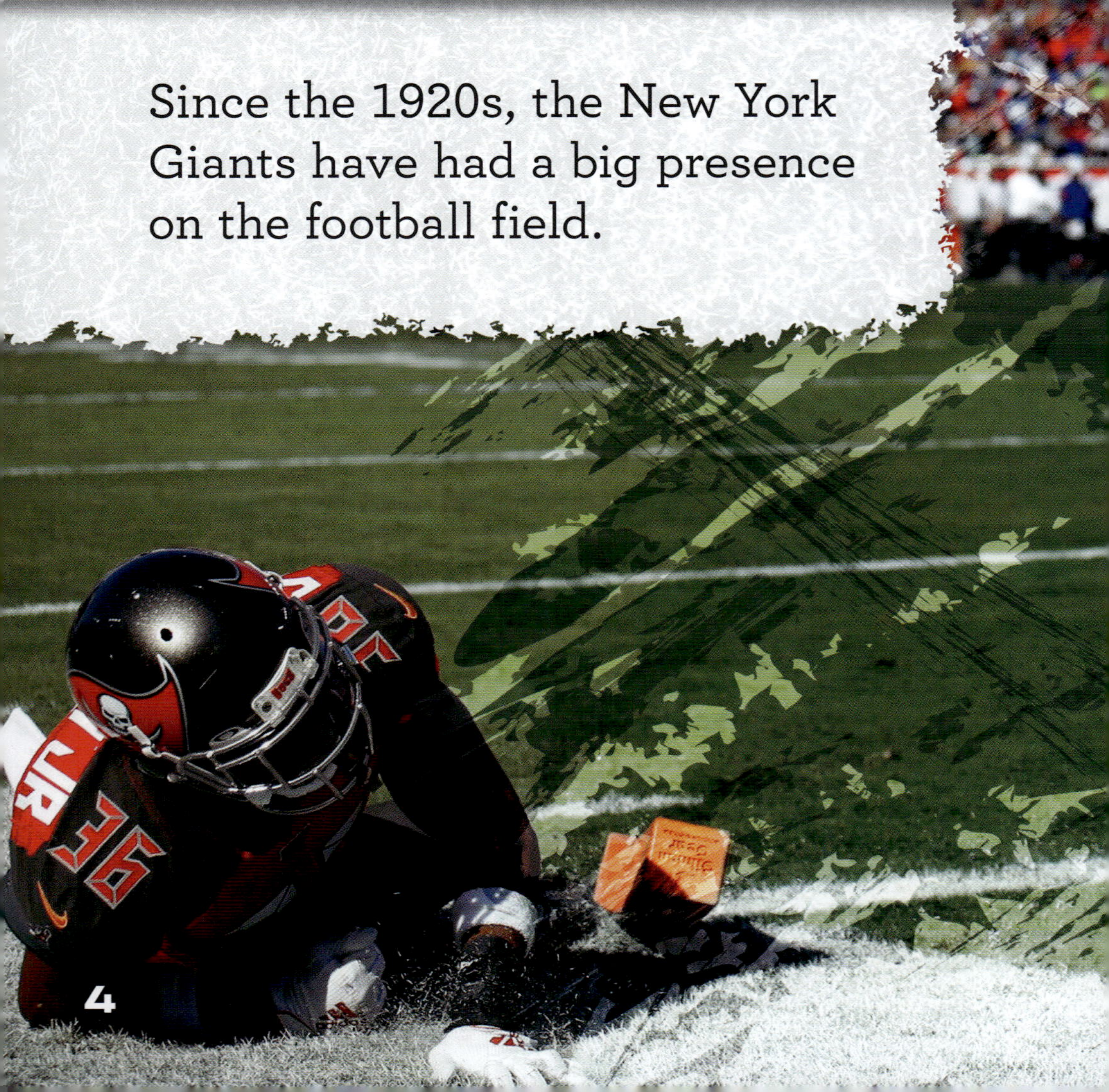

Nicknamed the "Big Blue Wrecking Crew," the Giants have toppled many teams for the win!

KICK OFF

The Giants were founded by Tim Mara in 1925. The team was important to the NFL's success. By being in the country's largest city, they brought the sport to many fans' attention.

In the Giants' third season, their powerful defense allowed only 20 points in 13 games! Their 11-1-1 record awarded them the NFL title.

The Giants were champions again in both 1934 and 1938. The team didn't win another **championship** until 1956. The Giants would go on to have just two winning seasons between 1964 and 1980. But things would get far better.

TEAM
RECAPS

The Giants won **Super Bowl** XXI in 1987. They beat the Denver Broncos 39–20. The team returned for Super Bowl XXV after the 1990 season. They beat the Buffalo Bills by just one point!

Ten years later, the Giants once again played in the Big Game. Unfortunately, they lost 34–7 to the Baltimore Ravens in **Super Bowl** XXXV.

The Giants made another **Super Bowl** appearance following the 2007 season. The game was tight. But they beat the **undefeated** New England Patriots 17–14! The Giants beat New England again four years later at Super Bowl XLVI.

SUPER BOWL CHAMPIONS
ny
Reebok
Star-Ledger
CHAMPS

Saquon Barkley had an incredible 2018 season. He rushed 261 times for 1,307 yards and 11 touchdowns. He also caught 91 passes. Barkley was named NFL Offensive **Rookie** of the Year.

The 2020 season was the first time the Giants played without its longtime **quarterback** Eli Manning since 2004. They ended with a 6-10 record, not qualifying for the playoffs.

HALL OF FAME

Mel Hein didn't miss a single game in his 15 seasons with the Giants. He was named the NFL's **MVP** in 1938. Hein is the only offensive lineman to win this award. Hein became one of the first members of the Pro Football Hall of Fame in 1963.

Mel Hein

Michael Strahan played for the Giants his whole career. He had 22.5 **sacks** in 2001, making the NFL single season record and was named the NFL's Defensive Player of the Year. He also went to the **Super Bowl** twice. Strahan was **inducted** into the Pro Football Hall of Fame in 2014.

Eli Manning became the team's starting **quarterback** in 2004. Manning led the team to two **Super Bowl** wins. He was named **MVP** in both games. Manning has the record for most passing yards in a single postseason, with 1,219. He was named the Walter Payton NFL Man of the Year in 2016.

GLOSSARY

championship – a game held to find a first-place winner.

induct – to admit someone as a member of an organization.

MVP – short for "most valuable player," an award given in sports to a player who has performed the best in a game or series.

quarterback (QB) – the player on the offensive team that directs teammates in their play.

rookie – a first-year player in a professional sport.

sack – when a quarterback is tackled behind the line of scrimmage while still in possession of the ball.

Super Bowl – the NFL championship game, played once a year.

undefeated – not having any losses.

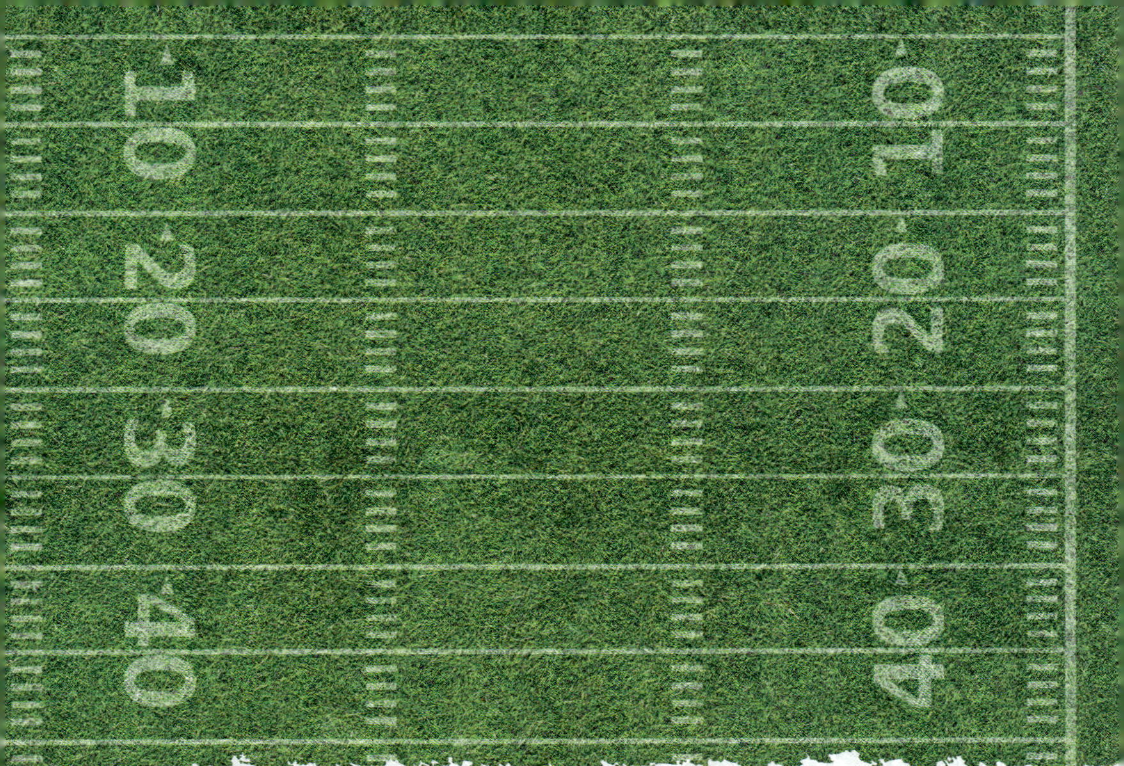

ONLINE RESOURCES

To learn more about the New York Giants, please visit **abdobooklinks.com** or scan this QR code. These links are routinely monitored and updated to provide the most current information available.

INDEX